Copyright © Cheryl Lee-White 2022

Cheryl Lee-White has asserted her right to be identified as the author of this Work in accordance with the Copyright, Designs and Patents Act 1988.

All rights reserved.

No part of this publication may be reproduced, stored in a retrieval system, or transmitted in any form or by any means, electronic, mechanical, photocopying, recording or otherwise, without the prior permission of the copyright owner.

www.cherylleewhite.co.uk

A catalogue for this book is available from the British Library

Dedication

This book is dedicated to everyone who is working hard to conquer their fears, gain courage and overcome adversity to achieve their dreams.

Contents

Achieve

Achieve	8
A Page of Your Life	9
Like the…	10
Not Just a Dream	12
Always There	13
Embark on a Journey	14
Reap What You Sow	15
The Seasons Will Change	16
Doubt is the Biggest Killer	18
That Takes Faith	20
Stand Up	22
Noes	23
Be That Person	24

Just Walk Away	25
Ticktok	26
Who Are You?	28
Fear	29
The Storm	30
Mountains Don't Apologise	31
The Best Listener	32
Conquering Your Mind	33
Be Like the Moon	34
Bring Others With You	35
The Power of Words	36
Release the Worry	37
The Large Oak Tree	38
Embrace the Silence	40
The Energy Sapper	41
Bloom Another Day	42
The Best Things Are Free	43

Self-Worth & Self-Love

Have the Courage	45
Your Worth	46
Time to Love Once More	47
Approval	48
Take Some Time	49
You Hate Your...	50
Stick it to Them	51
Doubt Talking	52
A Smile Is	54
Kind Words	55

Reflection

Overcoming the Dark	57
Your Fears	58
The Mask	60
Stepping Stones of Your Heart	62
A Trail Showing the Way	63
Dear Younger Self	64

Achieve

Achieve

Take a minute and believe,

Believe that you can achieve,

Achieve your highest goal,

A goal that enlightens your soul.

A Page of Your Life

A page of your life is starting anew,

And how it gets written is up to you.

Your life story you get to compose,

So make the decision and choose how it goes.

Like the...

Move like the ocean,

Putting actions into motion.

Be rooted like a tree,

Following the vision, you see.

Be strong like a bull,

And be unbreakable.

Spread like the weeds,

Sowing multiple seeds.

Work like a bee,

Doing things consistently.

Bloom like a flower,

Dazzling in your finest hour.

Glow like the sun,

Guiding others who have just begun.

Not Just a Dream

A dream is not just a dream,

Although imaginary at first, it may seem.

With hard work into life, it can be bought,

And become more than just a thought.

Always There

When you look up high,

In a cloud-filled sky,

And the sun is not in view,

It doesn't mean he is not there for you.

The sun will be there through clouds and rain,

Shining down on you just the same.

Doing his job, he will always be,

Even if what he does, you can't always see.

Embark on a Journey

Take those opportunities,

Not knowing where they will lead.

As you need to embark on a journey,

Before you can succeed.

Reap What You Sow

When things are simple,

Nothing will ever grow.

You need to put in the work,

To reap what you sow.

The Seasons Will Change

The seasons change every year,
Without fail, they will appear.

Mother nature in all her glory,
Embracing her ever-changing story.

Preparing for what is yet to come,
Be it rain, wind or the summer sun.

Riding the seasons as they arrive,

Making sure to flourish and thrive.

No complaining as change takes hold,

Instead, she prepares for what is to unfold.

Doubt is the Biggest Killer

Doubt is the biggest killer,

Scarier than any thriller.

Around every new bend,

It lies waiting to apprehend.

It will pull you apart from inside-out,

Spreading through your body self-doubt.

It will stop you in your tracks,

Making you believe it's untrue facts.

It stops you from carrying on,

Making sure your courage is all gone.

So don't let doubt take hold,

And these events over you unfold.

Be on the lookout for doubt,

And if you start to feel it, kick it straight out.

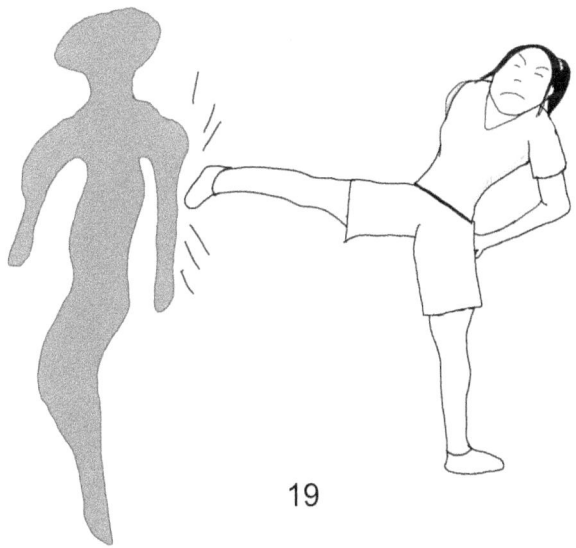

That Takes Faith

To walk the path unknown,

A way that has not been shown.

That takes Faith.

To blindly carry on through,

Not knowing what is ahead of you.

That takes Faith.

To keep going on your way,

Believing you will see a better day.

That takes Faith.

To bravely climb those mountains steep,

Slowly climbing them at a creep.

That takes Faith.

To pick yourself up after all the falls,

And carry on no matter what may befall.

That takes Faith.

Stand Up

Allow your beliefs to be shown.

Even if it means having to stand alone.

Sharing what you believe,

It may not always be well received.

It can be hard not to follow the crowd,

But find that courage to stand up proud.

Let your beliefs be your guide,

Helping you along on a tough ride.

Find that strength from deep within,

And keep going until you get that win.

Noes

Through life, you will hear those 'Noes',

And doors on you will get closed.

But for all those Noes that you go through,

There will be an open door just waiting for you.

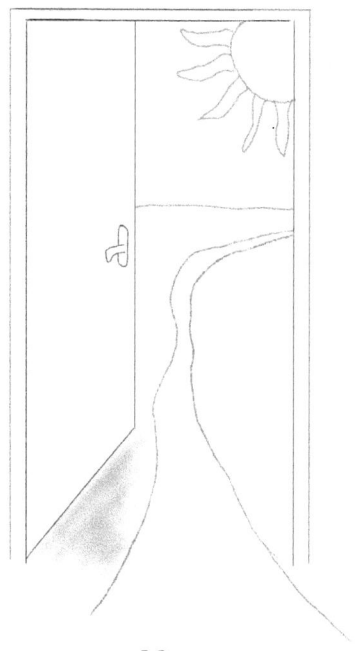

Be That Person

Be that person who lends a hand.

Be that person who helps other's plan.

Be that person who, to other's is kind.

Be that person who enriches the mind.

Be that person who stays strong.

Be that person who helps others carry on.

Just Walk Away

Sometimes the bravest thing you can do,

Is just to walk away.

It may seem hard at first,

But you'll feel better for it one day.

Ticktock

Ticktock,

Ticktock,

The ticking of the clock.

Time begins to fly,

With each second, that goes by.

Ticktock,

Ticktock,

The ticking of the clock.

The time will keep on turning.

As for more, you'll be yearning.

Ticktock,

Ticktock,

The ticking of the clock.

Hands that can't be rewound,

No extra time to be found.

Ticktock,

Ticktock,

The ticking of the clock.

Make those seconds count,

As your years begin to mount.

Who Are You?

Who are you?

Do you know?

Have you found your purpose?

And know which way to go?

Of these life's questions,

We often ask.

But finding the answers,

Can be a task.

But once you have found your purpose,

And know who you are.

Motivation will become easier,

And in life, you will go far.

Fear

From birth, fear into us is ingrained.

And when the going gets tough, fear can take the reins.

It tries to steer us back to comfort and safety,

But we need to think before being so hasty.

Is this fear we are feeling really justified?

Or is our body causing it to be amplified?

Listening to all our fears, can we really afford?

When conquering them could bring substantial reward.

The Storm

You can't control the storm,

Or when it will take form.

The chaos of it will unfold,

And you'll be forced to take hold.

So prepare for what is up ahead,

Calm yourself and don't fill with dread.

For this storm, you will need to ride,

But you'll come out stronger on the other side.

Mountains Don't Apologise

The mountains don't apologise,

For how hard they make the climb.

But once at the top,

They offer a beauty so divine.

The Best Listener

Sometimes the best listener,

Is a blank page.

It will listen to anything,

Whether happiness or rage.

Tell it about your problems,

Or deepest desires.

It will always be there for you,

And a pen is all it requires.

So fill that page,

Let everything out.

It will always listen to you,

Without a doubt.

Conquering Your Mind

Sometimes the biggest challenge isn't the mountain stood before you,

The biggest challenge is conquering your mind that is doubting you.

Be Like The Moon

Be like the moon,

Serene and bright,

Guiding others with your light.

Be like the moon,

Energetic and powerful,

Command oceans with your soul.

Be like the moon,

Humble and divine,

Helping others in the dark to shine.

Bring Others With You

When you are working hard,

And building up your throne.

Remember to bring others up with you,

Else you will find yourself alone.

The Power of Words

Words contain so much power.

The power to change you,

The power to help you grow,

The power to guide you,

The power to make imagination flow.

So pick up a book,

And grow one page at a time.

Expanding your mind,

With the power of every new line.

Release the Worry

We seem to worry about every little thing,

And with it a state of unrest it will bring.

In life, there is so much we can't control,

And worrying about these will torture your soul.

If it's out of your hands and there's nothing you can do,

Then release this worry from inside of you.

Put your focus on what you can change,

And only worry about things in this range.

This is a way to bring peace to your mind,

As worrying to the mind can be so unkind.

The Large Oak Tree

The large oak tree,

Holding on to her browning leaves.

Not ready to let them go,

To float off in the breeze.

The large oak tree,

To her leaves, she holds on tight.

Trying to slow their fall,

With all her might.

The large oak tree,

She slowly begins to see.

That trying to hold on,

Is not the way to be.

The large oak tree,

Finally, of her leaves, she is ready to let go.

As letting go of what no longer serves her,

Is the only way she can recover and grow.

Embrace the Silence

Don't avoid the silence,

It's not something to fear.

Let the silence surround you,

And calmness will appear.

Embrace the silence every day,

Immersing yourself in it whole.

Let it help to clear your mind,

And help enrich your soul.

The Energy Sapper

The energy sapper is waiting for you,

And draining your energy, he will do.

He comes in many forms and has many names,

But his task of sucking your energy remains the same.

if you feel your energy being drained away,

Then near the energy sapper, you can not stay.

Far away from him, you must go,

In order to protect your energy flow.

Bloom Another Day

When a forest fire rages on through,

Leaving a trail of destruction in its path.

The forest may look desolate,

But its destruction will not last.

For in the fire's wake,

The grass and flowers will find a way,

To grow and flourish,

And be ready to bloom another day.

The Best Things Are Free

The best things in life are free,

Just look around and you will see.

The air that you breathe,

The sunlight you receive.

Free!

The smiles that brighten your day,

The moonlight that guides the way.

Free!

The beauty of the sun on its depart,

The love of others that fills your heart.

Free!

Self - Worth & Self - Love

Have the Courage

Have the courage to love yourself for who you are.

You have the strength of the ocean and the heart of a star.

Feel the strength within and let it ripple through to your shore,

And let your light shine and guide you forevermore.

Your Worth

Your worth is not something that comes from,

Make-up,

Money,

Or Clothes.

It comes from within you,

And with Gratitude,

Happiness,

And a Smile,

It shows.

Time to Love Once More

Feel those sparks as they begin to fly,

As you look into those deepened eyes.

Let that desire in your soul ignite,

And love once again shine bright.

Look deep into those familiar eyes,

Deep enough until you realise.

That this love has been here once before,

And it's time to love the person in the mirror once more.

Approval

If approval from others is what you seek,

Then happiness it will never bring.

Seeking out your own approval,

Is the most important thing.

Take Some Time

You need to take some time,

To slow down and unwind.

You can't always be on the go.

Trying to help everyone you know.

By sitting down and putting up your feet,

You are not admitting defeat.

You are taking a well-needed rest,

So you can then carry on at your best.

You Hate Your...

You hate your hips,

You hate your thighs,

Your hair's too curly,

And you hate the colour of your eyes.

You want to feel better,

And want these to change.

So you look at your body,

When it's your thinking you should rearrange.

If your mind thinks you're ugly,

This is what your eyes will see.

But if you tell yourself you're beautiful,

Then beautiful is what you'll be.

Stick it to Them

Stick it to them!

The ones that put you down,

Made you frown,

Said you weren't enough.

The ones that made you tough.

Stick it to them!

The ones that tried to stop you,

To break you,

To make you suffer,

The ones that made you tougher.

Doubt Talking

"Everything is going to go my way."

"Are you sure you said the same yesterday?"

"I have a feeling that today will be good."

"I think that feeling has been mis-understood."

"I am sure today will go well."

"Well, yesterday didn't end so swell."

"I know, but I am staying positive, and today is a new day."

"A new day that will probably end in the same way."

"I am not listening to you, anyway what do you know?"

"Well, I am your self-doubt, and you're letting me grow."

"I am not listening anymore and I am getting rid of you."

"What, who else will doubt you and make you feel blue?"

A Smile Is...

A smile is a gesture so small,

And it cost nothing at all.

You may feel it isn't worthwhile,

But oh, the things you can do with a smile.

A smile is a happiness beam,

Letting happiness flow just like a stream.

It touches the hearts of others in a way,

That can help brighten up their day.

A smile is worth more than any gold,

It will keep your heart from turning cold.

Keeping that warm happiness flowing within.

So be sure to wear your warming cheerful grin.

Kind Words

Make your words kind,

And you will surely find,

The power they possess,

With the positivity they express.

Spread your kindness and before you know.

Others will spread their kindness, wherever they go.

Happiness

Love

Peace *Achieve*

Wonderful *Joy*

Reflection

Overcoming The Dark

The dark used to be a place of fear,

A place you wanted to steer clear.

But once you were pulled so deep inside,

You had to look within and find your stride.

You pulled yourself through,

And found better days were waiting for you.

Now the dark is not something you fear,

As you know, after the dark, light will appear.

Your Fears

Your fears tried to drown you,
But you carried on going.

Your self-doubt tried to engulf you,
But you carried on going.

Your anxiety tried to control you,
But you carried on going.

Your mind tried to stop you,
But you carried on going.

You carried on going,

Unsure of what was on the other side,

But despite it all, you carried on going,

And came out stronger on the other side.

The Mask

The mask you used to hide all these years,

To hide away your broken tears.

To hide away your pain and sorrow,

Whilst wishing for a better tomorrow.

The mask all these years you have worn,

Now lay tattered and torn.

Discarded on the floor,

Not needed by you anymore.

For you have grown,

Allowing your emotions to be shown,

You've discovered there's no need to hide.

That your raw unprocessed beauty from inside,

Was what the world truly needed to see.

And you, as you are, are now free to be.

Stepping Stones of Your Heart

Through all the tears that you've felt,

And the pain and heartache you've been dealt.

You searched deep and found the courage to carry on.

And through everything you faced you stayed strong.

Now, in the wake of all your pains and sorrows,

You have the courage to help others find better tomorrows.

Placing the stepping stones from your heart,

Helping guide others to the light and out of the dark.

A Trail Showing the Way

When you conquer that mountain,

You left behind,

A trail showing the way,

For others to find.

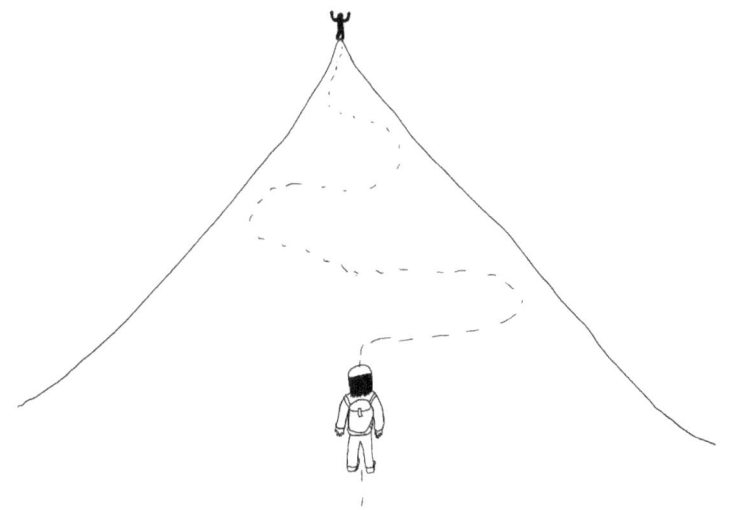

Dear Younger Self

Dear Younger Self,

You have been through so much,
But yet you have stayed strong.
Picking yourself up,
And carrying on.

For this, I must express,
An abundance of gratitude.
I wouldn't be where I am today,
Without your determined attitude.

I am a different person,

Different to you now,

This is because of you,

Growing and showing me how.

I am so thankful that you carried on

And your dreams you worked towards.

As for all your struggles,

I have received glorious rewards.

Love your Older Self

            X

*If you enjoyed reading **Achieve** why not read my other poetry book in the series **Believe**.*

Believe is an empowering poetry book to help change your perception.

A book of poems to motivate and inspire you whilst providing comfort and hope.

Available in ebook, paperback and hardback

Thank You for Reading My Book

If you have enjoyed reading this book, please consider leaving a short review on the retailer where you purchased it from.

Reviews not only mean the world to me and give me a confidence boost but they are also a way to find out what you liked about my poems. This helps me to write and produce future books that you will hopefully enjoy.

Reviews will also help my book to reach more readers.

Authors Note

I spend a few hours a week listening to motivational speeches, podcasts and reading self-help and empowering stories. Instead of listening to the radio or music, I will choose to listen to these empowering speeches whilst doing the cleaning, cooking or going from a run. I also read a bit every night before bed which a lot of the time is self-help books and memoirs. The current book I am reading now is 'Will' which is Will Smith's memoir and the book I read before that was 'Atomic Habits by James Clear.

Listening to and reading these types of inspirational stories has changed my life. They have taught me valuable lessons, empowered me and help give me the strength and tools to overcome hard times.

To help spread the messages of empowerment and positivity I have created my empowering poetry book series with 'Believe' and 'Achieve'. I would write down in the back of my notebook words, sentences, quotes or concepts that I heard that resonated with me and touched my soul. From these, I would expand on them, adding my own spin and style to these messages to create the poems in this book.

I hope that you found 'Achieve' helpful and that it injected a boost of empowerment and positivity into your day.

About The Author

Cheryl Lee-White is a best selling poet and award-winning children's author who lives in Somerset, England, with her partner and 3 daughters.

You can find out more at www.cherylleewhite.co.uk

Share Your Favourite Poem

Share your favourite poem over social media and tag me in on any of the following -

www.instagram.com/cherylleewhiteauthor

www.facebook.com/cherylleewhiteauthor

https://vm.tiktok.com/ZML82r1dJ/

Thank You!

www.ingramcontent.com/pod-product-compliance
Lightning Source LLC
Chambersburg PA
CBHW071541080526
44588CB00011B/1741